THE LIFE CYCLE OF A
Bee

By Colleen Sexton

BLASTOFF!
3
READERS

BELLWETHER MEDIA · MINNEAPOLIS, MN

Note to Librarians, Teachers, and Parents:

Blastoff! Readers are carefully developed by literacy experts and combine standards-based content with developmentally appropriate text.

Level 1 provides the most support through repetition of high-frequency words, light text, predictable sentence patterns, and strong visual support.

Level 2 offers early readers a bit more challenge through varied simple sentences, increased text load, and less repetition of high-frequency words.

Level 3 advances early-fluent readers toward fluency through increased text and concept load, less reliance on visuals, longer sentences, and more literary language.

Level 4 builds reading stamina by providing more text per page, increased use of punctuation, greater variation in sentence patterns, and increasingly challenging vocabulary.

Level 5 encourages children to move from "learning to read" to "reading to learn" by providing even more text, varied writing styles, and less familiar topics.

Whichever book is right for your reader, Blastoff! Readers are the perfect books to build confidence and encourage a love of reading that will last a lifetime!

This edition first published in 2010 by Bellwether Media, Inc.

No part of this publication may be reproduced in whole or in part without written permission of the publisher. For information regarding permission, write to Bellwether Media, Inc., Attention: Permissions Department, 5357 Penn Avenue South, Minneapolis, MN 55419.

Library of Congress Cataloging-in-Publication Data
Sexton, Colleen A., 1967–
 The life cycle of a bee / by Colleen Sexton.
  p. cm. – (Blastoff! Readers life cycles)
 Includes bibliographical references and index.
 Summary: "Developed by literacy experts for students in grades kindergarten through three, this book follows bees as they transform from eggs to adults. Through leveled text and related images, young readers will watch these creatures grow through every stage of life"–Provided by publisher.
 ISBN 978-1-60014-305-2 (hardcover : alk. paper)
 1. Bees–Life cycles–Juvenile literature. I. Title.
 QL565.2.S49 2010
 595.79'9–dc22
                            2009037215

Printed in the United States of America, North Mankato, MN.
010110   1149

Contents

Bees are **insects**. They live almost everywhere on Earth.

There are more than 20,000 kinds of bees. This bee is a honey bee.

Honey bees live in **hives**. They build wax **honeycombs** inside their hives.

A honeycomb has thousands of cells. Honey bees store food in some cells. They raise young bees in other cells.

Bees grow in stages. The stages of a bee's **life cycle** are egg, **larva**, **pupa**, and adult.

egg

larva

pupa

adult

A bee begins life as an egg in a honeycomb cell. The egg is white and the size of a grain of sand.

A larva hatches from the egg. A bee larva is called a **grub**.

grub

Adult bees feed the grub **royal jelly** and **beebread**. These special foods help the grub grow up healthy.

The grub eats and grows. The grub stops eating when it is fully grown.

It spins a case called a **cocoon** around its body. The grub has changed into a pupa.

A bee builds a wax cap on the cell. The pupa changes into an adult inside its cocoon.

The adult bee breaks out of the cocoon. It chews through the wax cap and leaves its cell.

Most adults are **workers**. These females
have many jobs. They clean, mend, and
protect the hive.

Workers care for grubs. They gather nectar and pollen from flowers for food. They make honey.

Some adults are **drones**. Drones are male bees. Their only job is to **mate** with a **queen bee**.

queen

Some adults are queens. There can be only one queen bee in a hive. New queens must fight each other for the job!

The queen leaves the
hive to mate with drones.
She is ready to lay eggs
when she returns.

The queen lays as many as 2,000 eggs every day! Each egg is the start of a new life cycle.

queen

Glossary

beebread—a mixture of honey and flower pollen that is food for worker grubs

cocoon—a hard case made of silk in which a pupa turns into a bee

drone—a male bee; a hive has about 100 drones.

grub—the larva of a bee

hive—a home for a group of bees; a hive holds honeycombs.

honeycombs—thousands of cells built of beeswax; the cells hold food, honey, and young bees.

insect—a small animal with six legs and a body divided into three parts; there are more insects in the world than any other kind of animal.

larva—a young insect that hatches from an egg and looks like a small worm; the larva is the second stage of a bee's life.

life cycle—the stages of life of an animal; a life cycle includes being born, growing up, having young, and dying.

mate—to join together to make young

pupa—the third stage of an insect's life when it turns from a larva into an adult; a bee pupa changes inside a cocoon.

queen bee—an adult female bee that lays eggs; a hive has only one queen bee.

royal jelly—a creamy food that comes from the head of a worker bee

worker—a female bee that gathers food, cares for the queen, and feeds the grubs; a hive has thousands of workers.

To Learn More

AT THE LIBRARY

Glaser, Linda. *Brilliant Bees*. Brookfield, Conn.: Millbrook Press, 2003.

Kalman, Bobbie. *Animal Life Cycles: Growing and Changing*. New York, N.Y.: Crabtree Publishing, 2006.

Sexton, Colleen A. *Honey Bees*. Minneapolis, Minn.: Bellwether Media, 2007.

ON THE WEB

Learning more about life cycles is as easy as 1, 2, 3.

1. Go to www.factsurfer.com.

2. Enter "life cycles" into the search box.

3. Click the "Surf" button and you will see a list of related Web sites.

With factsurfer.com, finding more information is just a click away.

Index

The images in this book are reproduced through the courtesy of: Bob Jensen / Alamy, front cover (adult), p. 8 (adult); Stephen Dalton, front cover (egg, pupa), pp. 8 (egg, pupa), 9, 13; Papilio / Alamy, front cover (larva), pp. 8 (larva), 10; blickwinkel / Alamy, p. 4; Nathan McClunie, p. 5; Dan Sullivan / Alamy, p. 6; Juan Martinez, p. 7; Juniors Bildarchiv, pp. 11, 17, 21; Gherasim Rares, p. 12; Florin Tirlea, p. 14; Heidi & Hans-Juergen Koch, p. 15; Irochka Tischenko, p. 16; Konrad Wothe, pp. 18-19; blickwinkel/ kottman / Alamy, p. 20.